First
Facts®

Your Favorite Authors

Kadir Nelson

by Lisa M. Bolt Simons

CAPSTONE PRESS
a capstone imprint

First Facts are published by Capstone Press,
1710 Roe Crest Drive, North Mankato, Minnesota 56003
www.mycapstone.com

Library of Congress Cataloging-in-Publication Data
Names: Simons, Lisa M. B., 1969– author.
Title: Kadir Nelson / By Lisa M. Bolt Simons.
Description: North Mankato, Minnesota : Capstone Press, 2017. | Series:
First facts. Your favorite authors. | Includes bibliographical references and index.
Identifiers: LCCN 2016023239| ISBN 9781515735564 (library binding) |
ISBN 9781515735618 (pbk.) | ISBN 9781515735656 (ebook (pdf)
Subjects: LCSH: Nelson, Kadir—Juvenile literature. | African American authors—Biography—
Juvenile literature. | African American illustrators—Biography--Juvenile literature. |
African American artists—Biography—Juvenile literature. | Authors, American—20th
century—Biography—Juvenile literature.
Classification: LCC PS3614.E44586 Z84 2017 | DDC 741.6/4092 [B]—dc23
LC record available at https://lccn.loc.gov/2016023239

Editorial Credits
Carrie Braulick Sheely and Michelle Hasselius, editors; Kayla Dohmen, designer;
Ruth Smith, media researcher; Gene Bentdahl, production specialist

Photo Credits
Alamy Images: Allstar Picture Library, 11 R, 13, Citizen of the Planet, 9 Mid; Associated
Press: Manuel Balce Ceneta, 15; Capstone Press: Michael Byers, cover, 17; Getty Images: Phil
Slattery/The Denver Post, 11 L; Newscom: Crissy Pascual/ZUMAPRESS, 19, Handout/MCT, 16,
Jeff Malet Photography, 21 Top; Photoshot: LFI, 5; Shutterstock: Beliavskii Igor, background
design elements, itlada, 7 Mid, Mega Pixel, 9 TR, mers1na, cover, neftali, 21 BL, Nuk2013,
cover, Olga Popova, 21 BR, Sean Pavone, 7 Top, Zadorozhnyi Viktor, 7 bottom

Printed in the United States of America.
092016   010030S17

Table of Contents

Chapter 1: Living a Dream

In 1996 Kadir Nelson got a job at a new movie company called DreamWorks. Nelson had graduated from college just weeks earlier. Nelson worked as a visual development artist for the movies, *Amistad* and *Spirit: Stallion of the Cimarron*. He created artwork to help develop the look of the movies. This was just the beginning of a successful career as an artist.

Nelson has received numerous awards for books he has illustrated and written throughout his career.

Chapter 2: An Early Start

Nelson was born in Washington, D.C., on May 15, 1974. At age 3 Nelson started drawing. When he started school, there were no art or music classes offered. But Nelson's uncle was an artist and art teacher. When Nelson was 10, his uncle made him an **apprentice**. Nelson's uncle taught him how to use **watercolors** and other art basics.

---

apprentice—a person who works for and learns from a skilled professional

watercolor—paint that is mixed with water

Nelson spent much of his childhood in San Diego, California. He graduated from Crawford High School.

"I've always been an artist. It's part of my DNA."—Kadir Nelson

DNA—material in cells that gives people their individual characteristics

As Nelson grew older, he learned to do oil paintings and other types of artwork. In high school Nelson won an art **scholarship** for college. He attended Pratt Institute in Brooklyn, New York. After he graduated, Nelson worked for several companies. He created art for Coca-Cola, Major League Baseball (MLB), and *Sports Illustrated.*

---

scholarship—money given to a student to pay for school

Pratt Institute

"There was a poster in my math class in high school, and it said, 'Wish upon a star ... but do your homework, too.' And that's kind of what I was doing by visualizing myself being successful at what I wanted to do. I was really kind of wishing upon a star, but I was also doing the work."—Kadir Nelson

Soon an editor asked Nelson to illustrate a children's book. *Big Jabe* by Jerdine Nolen was **published** in 2000. It tells the story of a young slave who finds a baby floating down a river in a basket. The baby grows very quickly and has amazing strength and powers. Actress and director Debbie Allen also asked Nelson to illustrate her books, *Brothers of the Knight* and *Dancing in the Wings*. These titles started Nelson's career as a children's book illustrator.

---

publish—to produce and distribute a book or other printed material so that people can buy it

Influencing Painters

Nelson says many artists have **influenced** his work, including Ernie Barnes. Barnes is known for the unique way he showed movement in his art.

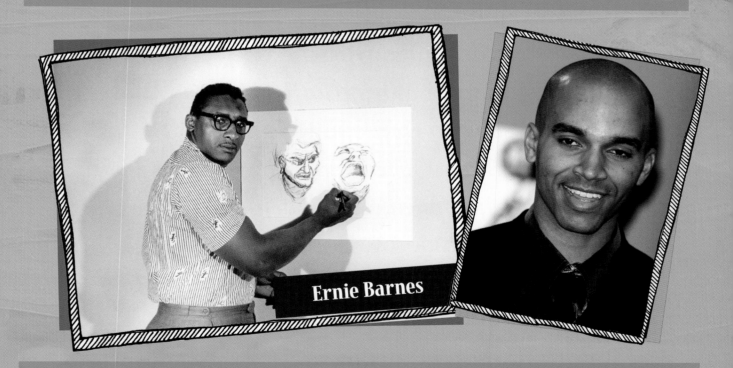

Ernie Barnes

influence—to have an effect on someone or something

Chapter 3: Hope and Nobility

Others noticed Nelson's work. Actor Will Smith and Director Spike Lee hired Nelson to illustrate their books.

Nelson continued working. He illustrated *Moses: When Harriet Tubman Led Her People to Freedom.* He also illustrated *Henry's Freedom Box: A True Story from the Underground Railroad.* Nelson won Caldecott Honors for these African-American history books in 2007 and 2008. The American Library Association gives this award for the best illustrated picture book each year.

Will Smith, his son Trey, and Kadir Nelson
at a book signing event

People collected Nelson's artwork as he became more famous. His work appeared in **galleries**, museums, and homes around the world. The Museum of African American History in Detroit, Michigan, and the Bristol Museum in England have displayed his work. His artwork also has appeared in national and international **publications**.

---

gallery—a place where art is shown

publication—something that has been printed and made available for people to buy

Portrait of a Pop Star

Music star Michael Jackson wanted a **portrait** of himself. He asked Nelson to paint one. Jackson died before Nelson started the project. He painted Jackson six years later.

Nelson shows his painting of former U.S. Representative Shirley Chisholm in 2009. Chisholm was the first African-American woman elected to the U.S. Congress.

portrait—a painting, drawing, or photograph of a person that only includes the person's head

In 2008 the first book Nelson wrote and illustrated was published. It's called *We Are the Ship: The Story of Negro League Baseball.* Nelson won the Coretta Scott King Author Award for the book. Nelson also won a Coretta Scott King Illustrator Honor for the title.

"My work is all about giving people a sense of hope and nobility. I want to show the strength and integrity of the human being and the human spirit."—Kadir Nelson

nobility—having or showing personal qualities that people respect

WE ARE THE SHIP
The Story of NEGRO LEAGUE BASEBALL

Words and Paintings by
KADIR NELSON

Nelson soon wrote and illustrated another book. In 2011 *Heart & Soul: The Story of America and African Americans* was published. Nelson won another Coretta Scott King Author Award for this title. He also won another Coretta Scott King Illustrator Honor. Nelson has written and illustrated other books, including *Baby Bear* and *If You Plant a Seed*.

Nelson spends countless hours focused on his work. His studio is in San Diego, California.

Chapter 4: Writing with a Goal

Whether writing or illustrating, Nelson keeps his goals in mind. He wants to create art that is real and interesting. He wants people to have strong feelings about his work. Nelson also believes he should share African-American history in some of his art. He wants his art to tell stories and have "human truth." He believes this will help people understand the artwork.

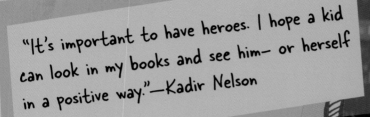

"It's important to have heroes. I hope a kid can look in my books and see him— or herself in a positive way."—Kadir Nelson

Kadir Nelson speaks at the National Book Festival in Washington, D.C., in 2011.

Nelson painted two portraits of basketball great Wilt Chamberlain. These portraits became stamps for the United States Postal Service in 2014.

Timeline

1974 born May 15 in Washington, D.C.

1996 graduates from Pratt Institute and gets hired at DreamWorks

1999 *Brothers of the Knight* is released

2000 first illustrated book, *Big Jabe*, is released

2003 becomes National Book Award Finalist for *Hush*

2004 becomes a Coretta Scott King Illustrator Honor winner for *Thunder Rose*

2005 wins Coretta Scott King Book Award for Illustrators for *Ellington Was Not a Street*

2007 wins Coretta Scott King Book Award for Illustrators and the Caldecott Honor for *Moses: When Harriet Tubman Led Her People to Freedom*

2008 first book that Nelson authored and illustrated himself is published, *We Are the Ship: The Story of Negro League Baseball*

2008 wins Caldecott Honor for *Henry's Freedom Box*

2009 wins the Coretta Scott King Award for Authors for *We Are the Ship: The Story of Negro League Baseball*

2012 wins the Coretta Scott King Book Award for Authors for *Heart and Soul*; is also a Coretta Scott King Illustrator Honor winner for same title

Glossary

apprentice (uh-PREN-tiss)—a person who works for and learns from a skilled professional

DNA (dee-en-AY)—material in cells that gives people their individual characteristics

gallery (GAL-uh-ree)—a place where art is shown

influence (IN-floo-uhnss)—to have an effect on someone or something

nobility (NOH-bil-it-ee)—having or showing personal qualities that people respect

portrait (POR-trit)—a painting, drawing, or photograph that only includes a person's head

publication (pu-bluh-KAY-shun)—something that has been printed and made available for people to buy

publish (PUHB-lish)—to produce and distribute a book, or other printed material so that people can buy it

scholarship (SKOL-ur-ship)—money given to a student to pay for school

watercolor (WAW-tur-kuhl-ur)—paint that is mixed with water

Read More

Fandel, Jennifer. *You Can Write Awesome Stories.* You Can Write. Mankato, Minn: Capstone Press, 2012.

Schwake, Susan. *Art Lab for Kids: 52 Creative Adventures in Drawing, Painting, Printmaking, Paper, and Mixed Media for Budding Artists of All Ages.* Beverly, Mass. : Quarry Books, 2012.

Internet Sites

FactHound offers a safe, fun way to find Internet sites related to this book. All of the sites on FactHound have been researched by our staff.

Here's all you do:

Visit *www.facthound.com*

Type in this code: 9781515735564

Index

Super-cool stuff! Check out projects, games and lots more at www.capstonekids.com